THE LIBRARY OF
AMERICAN
LIVES AND TIMES™

JAMES MADISON

Patriot, Politician, and President

David B. Mattern

The Rosen Publishing Group's
PowerPlus Books™
New York

For Ben, Blakely, Sam, Conor,
Michael, Luke, Joe,
Erik, Kim, Jenna
Katie and Lisa

Great kids all

Published in 2005 by The Rosen Publishing Group, Inc.
29 East 21st Street, New York, NY 10010

First Edition

Editor's Note: All quotations have been reproduced as they appeared in the letters and diaries from which they were borrowed. No correction was made to the inconsistent spelling that was common in that time period.

Library of Congress Cataloging-in-Publication Data

Mattern, David B., 1951–
James Madison : patriot, politician, and president / David B. Mattern.
   v. cm. — (The library of American lives and times)
Includes bibliographical references and index.
Contents: A Child of the Piedmont — The Revolution begins — A politician for life — "All men shall be free to profess"— What form of government is perfect? — Launching the ship of state — A noble acquisition — Walking the line — The United States stands up to Britain — Montpelier and retirement.
ISBN 1-4042-2648-6 (lib. bdg.)
1. Madison, James, 1751–1836—Juvenile literature. 2. Presidents—United States—Biography—Juvenile literature. [1. Madison, James, 1751–1836. 2. Presidents.] I. Title. II. Series.
E342 .M325 2005
973.5'1'092—dc22

                   2003017847

Manufactured in the United States of America

Introduction

When James Madison was born on March 16, 1751, thirteen British colonies had been established along the eastern coast of North America. From New Hampshire in the north to Georgia in the south, each colony was connected to Britain by ties of family, trade, and government. Yet there were few connections among the one million people who lived in these different colonies. A farmer who grew barley in Massachusetts and a plantation owner whose slaves grew rice in South Carolina had little in common except for the fact that they were both Englishmen living in North America.

By the time of James Madison's death on June 28, 1836, those thirteen colonies had been forged into one nation. They had become the United States of America, a nation composed of twenty-five states and a number of territories that stretched west from the Atlantic Ocean to the Rocky Mountains and north from the Gulf

Opposite: James Madison, painted by Charles Willson Peale in 1792, believed that a citizen's participation in government was essential if the government was to endure. In an 1829 letter, Madison wrote, "[M]en cannot be justly bound by laws, in making which they have no share."

of Mexico to the Canadian border. In 1836, about fifteen million Americans lived in what Madison's good friend Thomas Jefferson called the "Empire of Liberty." Each state sent representatives to Washington, D.C., a city that had been built as the capital of the new nation. The United States was a grand experiment in republican government, and its chief architect was James Madison.

James Madison was a key figure in the American Revolution and the early years of the American republic. He did not lead armies, nor did he negotiate treaties. Instead, he thought hard about what a government should be and he persuaded others to try his ideas. In James Madison's forty years of government service, as a revolutionary leader, a legislator, a secretary of state, and a U.S. president, he worked to fashion a government that was strong enough to protect its citizens and to guarantee their right to "life, liberty, and the pursuit of happiness."

The republic that Madison, along with his fellow revolutionaries, designed was a limited government that drew its power and authority from the people. This meant that it was a government whose laws were made by the people's representatives and not by a government based on the whim of one man, a monarchy, or of a group of men, an oligarchy.

Not only did James Madison help to design the American government but also he led the nation through its first great crisis, the War of 1812. Britain had sought to dominate U.S. trade and to reap financial and territorial advantages by defeating the United States. Under Madison's steady presidential leadership, the United States fought off the British challenge.

The story of James Madison's life is in some ways the story of our nation's founding. Although hundreds of thousands of men and women participated in the American Revolution, few people had as great an impact on the events of that period as did James Madison. Moreover, the republican government he helped to found was a great success and has lasted, with some revisions, to this day. This is James Madison's story.

1. A Child of the Piedmont

James Madison was the oldest child of James Madison Sr., a tobacco planter in Virginia, and Nelly Conway Madison, the daughter of a Virginian plantation owner. James grew up on a plantation called Montpelier in the Piedmont region of Virginia, about 30 miles (48 km) east of the Blue Ridge Mountains. Ambrose Madison, James's grandfather, had settled Montpelier in the 1730s. Ambrose, a merchant in the York River region of Virginia, had acquired about 2,300 acres (931 ha) of land by 1728. Ambrose died soon after bringing his family and slaves to live on the property. Frances Taylor Madison, James's grandmother, raised the children and ran the plantation.

In those early years, life was difficult for Virginians. Dense forests had to be cleared from the land and heavy red clay soil had to be plowed before corn and tobacco could be planted. Tobacco plants required a great deal of care. The seeds were sown in nurseries and the seedlings were transplanted at just the right time and then weeded constantly as they matured. At

This 1818 watercolor of Montpelier was created by the Baroness Hyde de Neuville. When the Madisons moved into their new family home around 1760, James assisted by carrying furniture from the old house to the new house. On Sundays the family left Montpelier to attend Brick Church, located some two hours away on horseback.

harvesttime, the plants' leaves were picked, carefully cured and dried, packed in barrels, and then transported to market, either by rolling the barrels along the roads or by loading them onto flat-bottomed boats. Tobacco provided a way to become rich in Virginia, but it required good management, hard work, and sometimes a measure of luck.

By the time James's father, James Madison Sr., took over the plantation, it was small but well established. Madison Sr. kept adding to his landholdings

This engraving illustrated an 1800 essay by William Tatham concerning the processing of tobacco for human use in the Tidewater region of Virginia. Shown are the curing, airing, and storage of tobacco leaves. Fresh leaves have a different odor and taste than processed leaves have.

and purchased additional slaves so he could grow more tobacco. He also built a large smithy, or forge, where skilled slaves produced iron items such as hooks, nails, horseshoes, and wagon wheels, which he sold to his neighbors. Before long James Madison Sr. was the principal landowner and slaveholder in Orange County, Virginia.

James Madison grew up on this bustling plantation. He was about nine years old when his family moved from the old, cramped wooden house at Mount Pleasant to the family's new two-story brick mansion, which sat

James Madison Sr. served as vestryman for the Brick Church. As vestryman he was responsible for hiring a minister and collecting church
taxes. He was also authorized to restrict members of his community
from cursing and from riding their horses on Sundays. Charles Peale
Polk painted this portrait of James Madison Sr. in 1799.

James was similar to his mother, Nelly Conway Madison, shown in a portrait from around 1799 by Charles Peale Polk, in that he frequently suffered from ailments and illnesses. Despite her maladies, Nelly Conway Madison lived to be ninety-seven.

about 1/2 mile (1 km) away on a ridge that faced the Blue Ridge Mountains. As a child James learned to ride horses, to hunt, and to fish.

A good part of James Madison's time was spent in a small, one-room schoolhouse on the plantation. There James, his brothers and sisters, and the neighboring children of other planters first learned to read, to write, and to do arithmetic.

James was a sickly child who periodically suffered, he later wrote, from "sudden attacks, somewhat resembling Epilepsy" throughout his life. These seizures, or nervous attacks, seemed to come on during times of stress and overwork. Madison was also prone to the many kinds of fevers that were present in the colonies, including malaria. He tried to avoid the Tidewater, or Virginia's marshy coastal regions, where fevers were particularly widespread during the humid summer months.

In 1762, when James was eleven, he was sent to the Innes plantation, about 70 miles (113 km) southeast of Montpelier in King and Queen County. There Donald Robertson, a Scotsman and a graduate of the University of Edinburgh, ran a school. Under Robertson's instruction, James learned Latin and Greek, as well as geometry, geography, history, and French. Robertson was an engaging schoolmaster and kindled in the young boy a lifelong love of learning. The five years James spent at that school were so important that later he would say of his old teacher, "All that I have been in life I owe largely to that man."

When James was sixteen, he returned to Montpelier. Most boys of his age began to work with their fathers to learn how to manage a plantation. However, it was clear to his parents that James had a special gift for learning. James spent the next two years studying with the Reverend Thomas Martin at home in Montpelier. Martin was the minister of Madison's local church and a recent graduate of the College of New Jersey at Princeton, which today is called Princeton University. He helped James prepare for his college entrance examinations.

Martin also suggested that Madison go to Princeton instead of the College of William and Mary at Williamsburg, Virginia, where most Virginians of

Madison's day attended school. Although New Jersey was far away, the Madisons decided that it would be a better choice than the College of William and Mary. They feared that James, who was already a frail boy, might not survive the fevers and diseases of the swampy Tidewater region. Furthermore, William and Mary's academic reputation had fallen. The college's best teachers had left, and it had been reported that a group of professors "played all Night at Cards in publick Houses in the City and were often seen Drunken in the Street." Such was not the kind of education the Madisons wanted for their promising young son.

2. The Revolution Begins

Sometime in the summer of 1769, James Madison saddled his horse and began the long journey to New Jersey. Madison was accompanied by his tutor, Thomas Martin, and by Sawney, a slave.

Madison rode past the familiar countryside of Virginian plantations into the unfamiliar landscapes of Maryland, Delaware, and Pennsylvania. The party took ferries over the Potomac, Susquehanna, Schuylkill, and Delaware rivers. The trip, which probably took two weeks, would have been an eye-opener for the young Virginian, especially when he reached Philadelphia, Pennsylvania.

Philadelphia was an enormous city for that time with a population of twenty-five thousand people. The residents of Philadelphia included people who were German, African, Scottish, Irish, and English. The Philadelphians bustled along the city's paved streets, ducking into red-brick shops and coffeehouses. They conducted business at the city's busy port on the Delaware River, where a forest of masts announced the presence of ships from around

This colonial-era engraving, based on a work by George Heap,
depicts the skyline of Philadelphia, Pennsylvania, from the east.
Landmarks such as Christ Church, whose tall steeple made the
church the era's tallest colonial structure, are highlighted in
the key at the base of the image.

the world. When James Madison traveled through
Philadelphia, the city was buzzing with protests
against British taxation. To the deep dismay of
Americans, Parliament in Britain had passed the
Townshend Duties, which were a series of taxes on
paint, paper, lead, and tea. Early protests would gain
momentum and eventually lead to the American
Revolution some years later.

When Madison finally reached Princeton, he said
good-bye to Thomas Martin and to Sawney and moved his

belongings into Nassau Hall, a three-story gray stone building that he would call home for the next three years. Madison did so well on his entrance exams that he bypassed the freshman class and began his studies with the sophomores. His teachers emphasized public speaking and the arts of argument and persuasion. Madison read the works of Greek and Latin authors in the original languages and studied modern writers such as Montaigne, Jonathan Swift, and Joseph Addison.

Madison kept a journal, which he filled with quotations from these and other favored writers. One line from Montaigne's essays that Madison took to heart and recorded was, "A Man should not delight in Praises that are not his due, nor be uneasy at Slander."

Most influential among Madison's professors was John Witherspoon, the president of the college. Witherspoon had trained as a minister in Scotland and was noted for his knowledge and for his ability to speak well in front of

John Witherspoon cautioned his students against vanity, as "nothing more certainly makes a man ridiculous than an over-forwardness to display his excellencies." His 1794 portrait by Rembrandt Peale was based on a 1787 work by Charles Willson Peale.

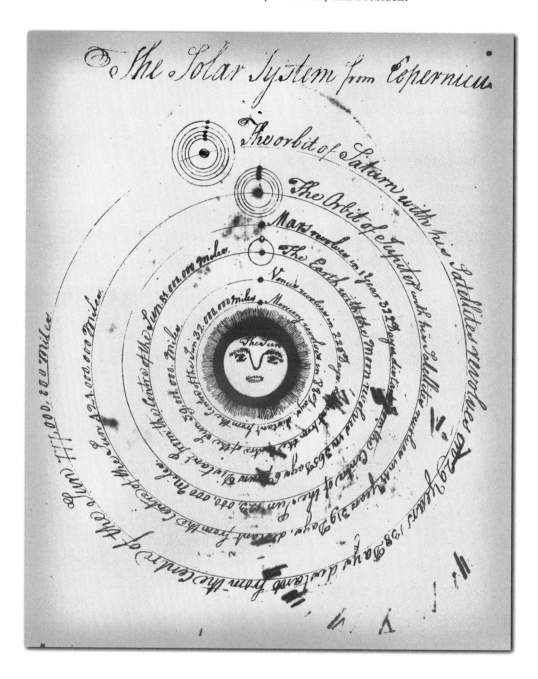

James Madison created this diagram, which he titled "The Solar System from Copernicus," during his junior or senior year at Princeton, sometime between 1770 and 1772. Nicolaus Copernicus was a sixteenth-century astronomer who theorized that the Earth and the other planets in the solar system revolve around the Sun.

others. He also was known for his suspicion of authority figures, both religious and secular. In Scotland, Witherspoon had written and spoken against the power that the Presbytery, or governing church authority, held over individual Presbyterian churches.

Madison completed his four years of college courses in two years, but he remained at Princeton for another year to study Hebrew and law. By that time he was exhausted and ill from his intense studies. He returned home to Montpelier in the spring of 1772 to recover and to consider what to do with his life.

James Madison was awarded this diploma from the College of New Jersey at Princeton upon his graduation. The document was decorated by a ribbon that was woven into the diploma. Melted wax was dripped onto the ribbon and stamped with a seal to authenticate the diploma.

Many of Madison's classmates taught school while they prepared to practice law or become ministers. Madison's closest friends at Princeton went on to distinguish themselves in government and literature. Eventually, Philip Freneau became a newspaper editor and a poet, Hugh Henry Brackenridge became a novelist, and William Bradford became a lawyer and attorney general of the newly formed United States.

At Montpelier James tutored his younger brothers and sisters and continued to read law books. He wondered whether he had the health and stamina to be a lawyer, which would require riding great distances to courts in the surrounding counties and spending long hours pleading his cases before large crowds. Or, if he chose instead to become a minister, could he overcome his natural shyness and preach to large congregations? Three years went by and Madison remained undecided.

While Madison considered what he might do, resentment toward Britain rose in every colony along the eastern seaboard. A group of Bostonians disguised as Native Americans had protested the British tax on tea by dumping chests that were filled with expensive tea from British ships into the Boston, Massachusetts, harbor on December 16, 1773. Britain retaliated against Massachusetts after this so-called Boston Tea Party by passing a series of Coercive Acts that closed the port of Boston in 1774. In response, the First Continental Congress, composed of representatives from almost every colony, met in Philadelphia in September 1774 to organize a united front against Britain.

That same year Congress agreed to boycott, or ban, the purchase of British imports and suggested that committees of safety be formed in every city, town, and county to enforce the measure. James Madison was appointed in December 1774 to the Orange County Committee of Safety, along with his father, who served as its chairman.

Orange County also focused on military preparedness, especially after the April 1775 battles at Lexington and Concord, which had been fought in Massachusetts. At Lexington and Concord, the British had tried to seize gunpowder and military stores from the local militia. The battles resulted in heavy British casualties, and Britain was determined to punish the Americans and reassert control over the colonies.

In October 1775, young James was appointed a colonel in the county militia. He drilled, marched, and practiced shooting with his countrymen. As a marksman, Madison considered himself to be average. On the likelihood of hitting a target the size "of a man's face at the distance of 100 yards," Madison wrote to his college friend William Bradford that, although he was "far from being the best," he could usually hit his target. Poor health, however, kept Madison from the full rigors of training, and he never fought on a battlefield.

In May 1776, James and his uncle William Moore rode for days in a pelting downpour to Williamsburg,

Virginia. The two men had been elected to represent Orange County in a convention that would create a new form of government for the colony of Virginia. Once the convention assembled, the first thing the delegates did was to instruct the Virginian members of the Continental Congress to propose a resolution for independence from Britain. Richard Henry Lee, a Virginian delegate at the Continental Congress, would present Virginia's resolution to the Continental Congress in June. After the Virginia resolution was approved by almost all the colonies, the Declaration of Independence would be signed in July 1776. Next the delegates at Williamsburg focused on the difficult task of drafting a plan for Virginia's government.

James Madison followed the discussions closely. At age 25, he was one of the youngest members of the convention and he served on a number of committees. One of these committees was assigned the task of debating what religious rights a Virginian should have.

Madison had long been angry about the treatment of local Baptists who had been jailed for preaching in the surrounding counties. Virginia had a state religion, Protestant Episcopal, and no one was allowed to preach without a state license. Only Protestant Episcopal ministers could get licenses. All Virginians, including Baptists and Quakers, paid taxes that were used to support the Episcopal Church. Furthermore, any Virginian who practiced a different faith, such as Judaism or

The Sentiments of the Baptists with regards to a General Assessment on the people of Virginia for the support of preachers of the Gospel; collected and agreed to, in an Association of Ministers and Deligates from the Churches of that persuasion, met at Dover in Goochland, the 25th of December 1776.

That "it is contrary to the principles of Reason and Justice "that any should be compelled to contribute to the Mainte-"nance of a Church with which their Consciences will not per-"mit them to join, and from which they can therefore recieve no "Benefit; is not merely the Opinion of the Dissenters (whose hardships on that score have feelingly convinced them of the Truth of it; but is the Declaration of the Hon. the General Af-sembly of Virginia. And we are happy to find the Progress of Liberty so far advanced that Legislature has passed "an Act for "exempting the different Societies of Dissenters, from contri-"buting to the support and maintenance of the Church as by, "law established, and its Ministers."

There is yet one undetermined point "touching the propriety of "a General Assessment, or whether every religious Society should be left to "voluntary Contributions for the support and maintenance of the seve-"ral Ministers and Teachers of the Gospel who are of different persuasions "and Denominations." And as our Representatives have "thought most "prudent to refer this matter to the discussion and final Determination "of a future assembly when the Opinions of the Country in general "may be better known; we look upon it to be not only an apology for, but a Call to us to publish our Sentiments with relation thereunto.

We believe that preachers should be supported only by voluntary Contributions from the people, and that a general assessment (how-ever harmless, and useful some may conceive it to be) is pregnant with various Evils destructive to the Rights and privileges of religious Society.

"No man or set of men are entituled to exclusive or seperate "Emoluments or privileges from the Community but in considera-"tion of public Services." If therefore, the State provides a Support

This petition against the General Assessment tax was drafted by the Virginia Baptist Association to the Virginia General Assembly on December 25, 1776. The Baptist ministers resented paying taxes on behalf of the Episcopal Church, the established church of Virginia. "We [the Baptist ministers] believe that preachers should be supported only by voluntary contributions from the people."

Catholicism, was barred from political office. Madison wrote to his friend William Bradford in 1774 that there were "in the adjacent County not less than 5 or 6 well meaning men in close [jail] for publishing their religious Sentiments . . . I have squabbled and scolded abused and ridiculed so long about it, to so little purpose that I am without common patience."

The committee deliberated on what religious rights a person should have and decided that "all Men shou'd enjoy the fullest Toleration in the Exercise of Religion." Although they agreed that the state of Virginia would tolerate the private practice of religions other than its own, worshiping in any church other than an Episcopal Church remained a privilege that could be taken away. Madison, who recalled the persecution of Baptists, suggested instead that "all men are equally entitled to the free exercise of religion, according to the dictates of Conscience." His change of wording meant that every person had a right to worship in the way that he or she wished. This right was a personal choice that could not be dictated by the government, nor could it ever be taken away.

Madison persuaded the committee to adopt this change and the convention later voted for it as well. The Virginia Declaration of Rights was the first important step toward a vital American principle, the separation of church and state. This was Madison's first, and perhaps greatest, contribution to American life.

3. A Politician for Life

James Madison was excited when he returned home from the Virginia convention in July 1776. Madison thought he had finally discovered what he would do with his life. He would not become a lawyer or a minister. Instead, he would become a politician, an elected official who represented his constituents wisely by making just and necessary laws. Elections were to be held the next spring for the legislature of the new state government.

To be a politician, however, one first had to be elected. In eighteenth-century Virginia, local elections were held in public at courthouses, and the candidates traditionally treated the voters to drinks of rum or whiskey. This custom was known as swilling the planters with bumbo.

Madison refused to treat his neighbors to alcoholic drinks and wrote that he found the practice to be "inconsistent with the purity of moral and of republican principles." The voters, however, thought that Madison was either too proud or too stingy to offer them beverages, and they elected his opponent.

Perhaps Madison learned from this experience and treated the voters to drinks from then on, for he never again lost an election.

During the 1776 convention, Madison had impressed a number of the delegates, and, when a vacancy occurred in the Virginian governor's council in November 1777, Madison was appointed to fill it. After taking his seat in January 1778, Madison began to deal with the day-to-day problems of running the American Revolution. As one of five councillors, Madison advised the governor on matters that ranged from providing supplies such as hogs, flour, and salt to the Continental army, to writing instructions for the state delegates to the Continental Congress on how to cast Virginia's vote. The governor and the council also handled appointments to state offices such as the militia and read petitions from Virginia's citizens. The council met six days per week, and Madison served for two years. During his term Madison learned the practical side of governing.

As a member of the governor's council, Madison also came to know Thomas Jefferson. The tall, lanky Virginian, already famous as the author of the Declaration of Independence, had been elected governor of Virginia in June 1779. In their daily council meetings, a friendship grew between the two men based on their mutual love of books and ideas and on their devotion to the American Revolution. Theirs would become one of America's greatest political collaborations and one of

America's deepest political friendships. When Jefferson died, Madison would recall that he had known his friend "for a period of fifty years, during which there was not an interruption or diminution of mutual confidence and cordial friendship, for a single moment in a single instance."

In December 1779, Madison was chosen by the Virginia legislature to represent Virginia in the Continental Congress. James Madison slogged through the heavy mud and rain to Philadelphia and served in the Congress for almost three and one-half years. Madison began to think about what was best for the country as a whole, rather than focusing only on what was best for

The leaders of the Continental Congress were later depicted by Augustus Tholey in 1894. Shown from left to right are John Adams, Gouverneur Morris, Alexander Hamilton, and Thomas Jefferson. The delegates are shown at work with their papers, ledgers, and rolled parchment strewn across the desk and floor.

Virginia. The problems that he and his colleagues faced at the national level were similar to what Madison had faced in Virginia, just on a larger scale. Instead of worrying that his state provide the Continental army with the requested supplies, he was now concerned that all the states honor their commitment to furnish the much-needed provisions. Madison had to ensure that a steady stream of food, clothing, and horses reached General George Washington's army, that officers and private soldiers were paid, and that relations with foreign countries worked to the advantage of the United States.

When Madison took his seat in Congress in March 1780, he was 29 years old and the youngest member of that body. One delegate who saw the short, slight man wrote to his wife that "young Mad[i]son" looked as if he were "just from the College." Before long, however, Madison proved to the other delegates that he was not a schoolboy. He worked hard at his committee assignments and was often chosen to write its reports. Madison would diligently prepare for the next day's session and often read late into the night. He did not speak often on the floor of Congress. Madison preferred to present his knowledge of the issues and his talent for argument in small committees where his words could do the most good. When he did speak in Congress, Madison was brief and to the point. Soon he was being chosen to sit on important committees and became known as one of the most reliable and influential members of Congress.

Madison joined the Congress during the darkest hours of the American Revolution. In May 1780, the British had captured Charleston, South Carolina, along with the entire southern Continental army. When another army of Continental soldiers, hastily put together, marched south in July, British troops defeated them at Camden, South Carolina. The Americans feared that the British would be able to cut off Georgia, South Carolina, and North Carolina from the rest of the Union. In September the American military hero General Benedict Arnold betrayed his country by attempting to turn over the fort of West Point, New York, to the British. Arnold's treason shocked and angered the country.

Worst of all, however, was the financial situation of the country. For years Congress had been issuing paper money called Continentals. By 1780, Congress had printed so many paper bills that they had become worthless in the eyes of the merchants and farmers who sold supplies to the states. As there wasn't enough gold or silver in the treasury to back these paper bills, the paper bills were considered valueless, or "not worth a Continental," as the eighteenth-century saying went. Additionally, Congress did not have the power to tax either the states or the people in order to raise funds for the treasury.

Because Congress had no income, it relied on contributions from the states. Although each state was

This Continental currency was printed in Philadelphia, Pennsylvania, on January 14, 1779. The leaf design, or nature print, on the back of the bill was intended to deter counterfeiters. The design was created from a leaf that was pressed into plaster. This plaster impression was then cast into a metal mold. Every leaf is unique and therefore hard to copy.

supposed to give Congress money and supplies to help run the country and the war, the state governments often ignored these requisitions. The state governments had their own financial problems. Without money, Congress found it impossible to pay or to feed the army or to do any of the necessary tasks that governments are formed to do.

To fill the treasury, American diplomats approached France and Holland for loans. Madison and his colleagues also tried to devise a tax plan that would be acceptable to all the states. According to the Articles of Confederation, a document adopted by Congress in 1781 to unite the colonies and give structure to the Union, the articles could only be amended if all the states agreed. In 1783, Congress passed an amendment that provided for an import tax. A tax of 5 percent would be levied on all imported goods and the proceeds would provide the national government with an income. When Congress sent the amendment to the states for approval, Rhode Island, the smallest state, defeated the measure.

Thanks to foreign loans, and to help from the French army and navy, and to the loyalty and endurance of the Continental army, American troops finally defeated the British at Yorktown, Virginia, in 1781. The British signed a peace treaty with the United States in 1783, bringing a successful close to the military part of the American Revolution. When

Madison left Congress for Virginia at the end of his term that same year, he worried about the weakness of the national government. The war had been won, but could the country remain united and survive?

4. Freedom of Religion

When James Madison returned to Montpelier in December 1783, he had earned a national reputation as one of Virginia's strongest leaders. His Orange County neighbors voted him into the Virginia legislature in 1784 and again in 1785 and in 1786.

Thomas Jefferson, who had been working on a revision of Virginia's laws, had been appointed U.S. minister to France. Jefferson asked Madison to work in the legislature to gain passage of his revised code of laws while he was gone. James Madison worked hard on this task and many laws were changed to reflect Jefferson's ideas.

In the 1784 session of the Virginia legislature, Patrick Henry, the famous orator, introduced a bill for a tax to support teachers of the Christian religion. The bill would have created, in effect, a state religion by requiring all taxpayers to support the Christian religion. Madison and others negotiated to get the bill postponed. By June 1785, Madison had written a petition to the Virginia General Assembly called

Patrick Henry was a Virginian lawyer who later became a member of the House of Burgesses. George Cooke's painting from around 1834 dramatizes Henry arguing a case in the Hanover County Courthouse in Virginia in 1763. Henry's father, moved by his son's passionate speech, stands beneath the left window, crying into a red handkerchief.

"Memorial and Remonstrance against Religious Assessments," in which he made his case against Henry's bill.

Madison explained in his petition that religious liberty was an inalienable right and that the state, meaning the governor or another state official, had no right to intervene in religious matters. If the state could tax every Virginian on behalf of Christian teachers, then, under the same principle, the government could require that everyone practice the same religious faith. Just look at Europe, Madison wrote, where wars had been fought for centuries between one religious sect and another, and "torrents of blood had been spilled." Did Americans want to fight those same battles?

James Madison circulated his "Memorial and Remonstrance" petition and the document was signed by more than 1,500 people. After more than 10,000 people signed several petitions against Henry's bill, the bill was overwhelmingly defeated. Sensing that the time was right, Madison promoted one of Jefferson's proposed laws, the Statute Establishing Religious Freedom. The General Assembly passed it into law in 1786. In Virginia, at least, it became the law that "all men shall be free to profess, and by argument to maintain, their opinions in matters of religion."

Every fall from 1784 to 1786, Madison traveled north to Philadelphia and New York. In the big cities, he would greet old friends, go to bookshops, attend plays, and, above all, discuss the sad prospects of the United States. Things were going badly. The United States was deeply in debt. The country owed money to the veterans of the Continental army and to those individuals who had invested in government bonds. The nation also needed to repay the huge loans from Holland and France. The United States could not even pay the interest on these debts, which meant that the nation could not apply for additional loans.

James Madison drafted this page of his "Memorial and Remonstrance against Religious Assessment" in the summer of 1785. Madison wrote to Edward Livingston many years later on July 10, 1822, "I have no doubt that every new example will succeed, as every past one has done, in shewing that religion and Government will both exist in greater purity the less they are mixed together."

Moreover, because the national government was so powerless, each state was beginning to act on its own. New York had sent trade negotiators to foreign countries to work out commercial treaties that would benefit only New York. States were printing their own paper money. Some states were protecting their own interests by charging citizens of other states for the right to use their ports, as though these Americans were foreigners. Other states were taxing their own citizens heavily to pay off state debts. All the states were ignoring the Congress and its pleas for funds.

At Montpelier, Madison thought about the problems the United States was facing. He was curious about whether republics in the past had faced these same problems, and, if they had, how they had resolved them.

To investigate this question, Madison opened a trunk of books that Jefferson had sent him from Paris, which included Diderot's famous *Encyclopédie*. Madison read deeply into history and studied examples of past republics. Each one had flourished for a time and then fallen into ruin. What had caused their downfall? How could something similar be prevented in the United States? Madison wrote down these thoughts in his "Notes on Ancient and Modern Confederacies."

Then Madison reflected on the situation of the United States. Incorporating his study of past republics, what he had heard from other citizens, and

A republic is a government in which the people hold supreme power. The people elect representatives who govern according to law, and who are responsible to the people for their actions.

Few republics existed before the United States. One ancient Greek republic that Madison studied was the Amphyctionic Confederacy, which began in 1522 B.C. and lasted until it was conquered by Philip II of Macedonia, the father of Alexander the Great.

According to Madison, this confederacy failed because it could not prevent the allied states in the confederation from going to war with one another. Although there were laws against such conflicts, the laws were not enforced. When the larger states bullied the smaller states, the smaller states never received justice.

his own observations, James Madison wrote "Vices of the Political System of the U.S."

Madison thought about the design of a new type of republic, one that would preserve the liberties of the people while still providing the government with enough power to be effective. When Americans were ready to discuss changes to their government, and they would be soon enough, James Madison would be ready.

5. What Form of Government Is Perfect?

James Madison was not alone in worrying about his country's future. Madison attended a national meeting that was held in Annapolis, Maryland, in September 1786 to discuss commercial relations between the states. Nothing was accomplished because not enough states sent representatives. Madison, Alexander Hamilton, and a number of other delegates called for another meeting to be held in Philadelphia the following summer to consider how the Articles of Confederation might be amended to solve the nation's problems.

That winter Madison was reelected to Congress. In January 1787, as Madison set off for a meeting of Congress in New York, fighting over taxation and debts had broken out in western Massachusetts. Farmers who were deeply in debt and struggling to pay heavy state taxes had shut down the courts and had marched to the armory in Springfield, Massachusetts. A government army met the farmers and defeated them.

Shays's Rebellion, as the uprising was called, was a threat not only to Massachusetts but also to the government of every state in the Union. If ordinary citizens were so unhappy that they took up arms against the state, changes needed to be made. Congress, however, was powerless to intervene. Although Massachusetts had put down the rebellion, influential citizens looked forward to the Philadelphia convention during which a lasting solution to the country's woes might be found.

James Madison arrived in Philadelphia in early May, some weeks before the convention was to begin. Even though the convention had been called simply to amend the Articles of Confederation, Madison had drafted a plan for a new government. Madison spent time talking to delegates as they arrived, discussing ideas and hopes for the meeting. In addition, Madison revealed his own plan to the delegates from Virginia and won their acceptance of his ideas. The Virginian delegates agreed that the governor of Virginia, Edmund Randolph, would present Madison's plan to the convention.

The Virginia Plan proposed a national government made up of three branches: executive, legislative, and judiciary. The president, the Congress, and the Supreme Court would run these three branches, respectively. This national government would have separate powers that, in theory, would not conflict with the powers of the states. Each branch would check the powers of the other branches. This separation and balance of powers would guard against one branch becoming too powerful. The combination of the federal government and the states exercising different powers was what James Madison called a mixed government.

The Constitutional Convention opened on May 25, 1787. Madison took a seat near the front and began to take notes. He recorded speeches and votes as accurately as he could. Madison revised and expanded these notes each night. Although he was not asked to do this, he considered a detailed record of the proceedings to be of great importance for future generations. Madison said

This was George Washington's copy of the Virginia Plan for the U.S. government. The plan was presented at the May 1787 Constitutional Convention. Washington may have jotted down Madison's ideas when the Virginian delegates first discussed Madison's proposal.

Next spread: This painting of the 1787 Constitutional Convention was created by Thomas Pritchard Rossiter around 1872. James Madison did not miss a single day of the convention. He tried not to step away for even an hour so that he could record every speech.

later that the task nearly killed him. His "Notes of Debates in the Federal Convention of 1787," published after his death, remain the most complete record of the convention's proceedings.

Four days later Edmund Randolph proposed the Virginia Plan. When the delegates adopted the plan as the basis for discussion, it was clear that they had decided to create a new form of government, not just a reworking of the old. There, however, agreement ended. A heated and exhausting debate began, which lasted all summer. James Madison spoke confidently and frequently during these discussions.

Each branch of the proposed government generated arguments. For the executive branch, some delegates wanted a presidency consisting of three men, while others thought that one individual was sufficient. Some wanted the president to be elected every year, while others for a six-year period, and still others for life. Questions arose as to what powers and qualifications a president should have, and how he should be elected.

The greatest debates revolved around the legislative branch. The delegates decided on a two-chambered Congress consisting of a House of Representatives and a Senate. What, however, would be the basis of representation in each chamber? Should representatives and senators be chosen by the states or by the people? How many representatives and senators should each state have? Should small states have as many representatives as larger states? Additionally, what powers should each chamber of Congress have?

When it was proposed that the smaller states would have fewer representatives, the delegates of the small states, such as Delaware, New Jersey, and Connecticut, threatened to walk out. Finally, a compromise was reached. The Senate would have two senators from each state regardless of the state's size. The number of each state's members in the House of Representatives, however, would be based on that state's population.

James Madison was disappointed in the outcome. He wanted proportional representation based on the state's population in the Senate as well as in the House. Long after the convention was over, Madison wrote that "the problem to be solved is, not what form of Government is perfect, but which of the forms is least imperfect."

Madison's presence seems to have had a calming effect in the assembly, for although he argued his points stubbornly he did so without offending anyone. One delegate from Georgia wrote that Madison "blended together the profound politician, with the Scholar . . . [He is] a Gentleman of great modesty, with a remarkable sweet temper."

After the convention ended in September 1787, Madison returned to New York. The draft of the U.S. Constitution was sent to the states for ratification, or approval. Nine states had to ratify the Constitution in order for it to become the new national government.

John Trumbull's painting of Alexander Hamilton was finished in 1805. Hamilton helped to found both the Bank of New York and the New York Stock Exchange.

Alexander Hamilton, a prominent congressional delegate from New York, thought that the various elements of the new Constitution needed to be explained to the people. Many citizens feared a strong federal, or national, government and worried that it would take away some basic rights of the citizens and the states.

Hamilton set out to write a series of newspaper essays that would inform the public and persuade them to endorse the new Constitution. Hamilton asked John Jay, the secretary of foreign affairs of the Congress, and James Madison to contribute essays. Jay wrote five essays, Madison wrote twenty-nine essays, and Hamilton wrote fifty-one essays. These essays were written quickly, and Madison recalled that in one case he was still writing the end of his essay while the printer was setting the beginning paragraphs in type. The eighty-five essays were collected and published in 1788 as *The Federalist*.

In March 1788, Madison went home to defend the Constitution in the Virginia Ratifying Convention. Many people in his home state disliked the new frame of government. They were called Antifederalists and Patrick Henry was their leader. Henry thought the new government would be too powerful and would intrude on the rights of the people. There was no bill of rights, Henry said, and nothing to guarantee an individual's right to a trial by a jury. Nor were there any safeguards to protect an individual's property from search and seizure by the government.

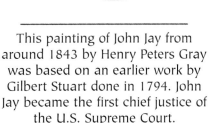

This painting of John Jay from around 1843 by Henry Peters Gray was based on an earlier work by Gilbert Stuart done in 1794. John Jay became the first chief justice of the U.S. Supreme Court.

Patrick Henry was a great orator, a man who could make his listeners feel anger or sorrow by the expressive delivery of his words. In the Virginia Ratifying Convention, Henry spoke for hours. Each time Henry finished a passionate speech, Madison would rise and calmly point out the flaws in Henry's argument. Madison patiently explained that the new federal government would have limits on its powers and that Virginia would retain most of the powers that it had always had. Madison also pointed out the advantages that the new government would bring, such as respect from foreign countries, a sound currency, and a strong union.

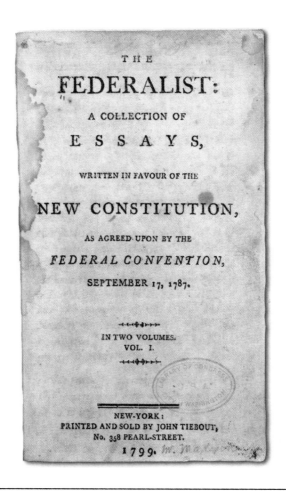

THE

FEDERALIST:

A COLLECTION OF

E S S A Y S,

WRITTEN IN FAVOUR OF THE

NEW CONSTITUTION,

AS AGREED UPON BY THE

FEDERAL CONVENTION,

SEPTEMBER 17, 1787.

IN TWO VOLUMES.
VOL. I.

NEW-YORK:
PRINTED AND SOLD BY JOHN TIEBOUT,
No. 358 PEARL-STREET.
1799.

This is the cover from the 1799 edition of *The Federalist*. According to Madison, the pace at which the *Federalist* essays were written and then printed in newspapers was so fast, the authors could not have their work reviewed before the essays were published.

Madison and the other supporters of the Constitution were successful. After a long debate, the Constitution was adopted in Virginia by a vote of 89–79. By the end of June 1788, ten states had approved the new Constitution, enough to put it to work.

6. Launching the Ship of State

A government mapped out on paper is one thing, but how that government actually works in reality is another matter. Elections were the next crucial step. Everyone thought that the great Revolutionary War commander George Washington should be president and he was, in fact, elected unanimously. The elections for the House of Representatives and the Senate, however, were hotly contested. In Virginia, the legislature chose the state's U.S. senators. Patrick Henry, who was then governor of Virginia, used his influence with the Virginia General Assembly to block James Madison's election to the Senate, and two Antifederalists were elected instead.

James Madison ran for a seat in the House of Representatives. The district he wished to represent included Orange, Spotsylvania, Amherst, Louisa, and Culpeper counties. His opponent in the campaign was his friend James Monroe. Monroe, running as an Antifederalist, was a veteran of the American Revolution and a former delegate to the Continental Congress.

There were many voters in the district who thought that Madison had spent so much time in Philadelphia and New York that he had lost touch with the people of Virginia. Virginia's voters were frightened by the potential powers of the new government and alarmed that there was no bill of rights to safeguard their individual freedoms.

During a harsh winter, the two candidates Madison and Monroe toured courthouses and churches to bring their cases for candidacy to the people. One icy day in Culpeper County, Madison got a mild case of frostbite when he delivered his speech outdoors.

When James Madison ran for election to the House of Representatives in 1789, he may have campaigned outside a courthouse such as the one shown here. The Gloucester County Courthouse in Virginia was built in 1766.

Although Madison disliked speaking in front of large groups, he overcame his anxiety and was able to explain the advantages of the new Constitution. After listening to people's concerns, he came to recognize the importance of a bill of rights. Madison promised that, if elected, he would secure one.

James Madison was elected to the House of Representatives in February 1789. He began serving in April, when Congress finally convened.

The U.S. Constitution provided the bare bones of government and authorized an executive, a legislative, and a judiciary branch. The document did not say, however, how these branches of government would be run. For example, beyond the president and vice president, who was to do the work of the executive branch? How many justices should there be on the Supreme Court? Should there be other federal courts? As Madison wrote to Jefferson, who was still in Paris, "We are in a wilderness without a single footstep to guide us." The framework had to be transformed into a working government.

Madison took the lead in this work. Fisher Ames, a representative from Massachusetts, explained to a friend why Madison's guidance was so often heeded: "He is possessed of a sound judgement, which perceives truth with great clearness, and can trace it through the mazes of debate, without losing it. . . . He is a studious man, devoted to public business, and a thorough master of almost every public question that can arise, or he will spare no pains to become so."

The First Federal Congress, the first congress that convened under the U.S. Constitution, was held between April 8 and September 29, 1789. This Congress established a revenue system based on the taxation of imported goods and created the executive departments of state, treasury, and war to help the president carry out his duties. Congress also decided on a permanent residence for the federal government, to be located on the banks of the Potomac River, or what is present-day Washington, D.C. Most important of all, the delegates agreed on a number of proposed amendments to the Constitution, which they passed on to the states for ratification.

To arrive at these proposed amendments, Madison had whittled down about two hundred suggested amendments that had been collected in Congress to nineteen amendments. Congress chose twelve to send to the states, and ten were finally ratified. These first ten amendments to the U.S. Constitution became known as the Bill of Rights. Among them are freedom of speech and of religion, the right to a trial by jury, and the right to assemble peacefully. Madison had fulfilled his promise to the people of his district.

The first session of the First Federal Congress was a success. However, there was trouble in the Washington administration. The president had chosen Alexander Hamilton as his secretary of the treasury and Thomas

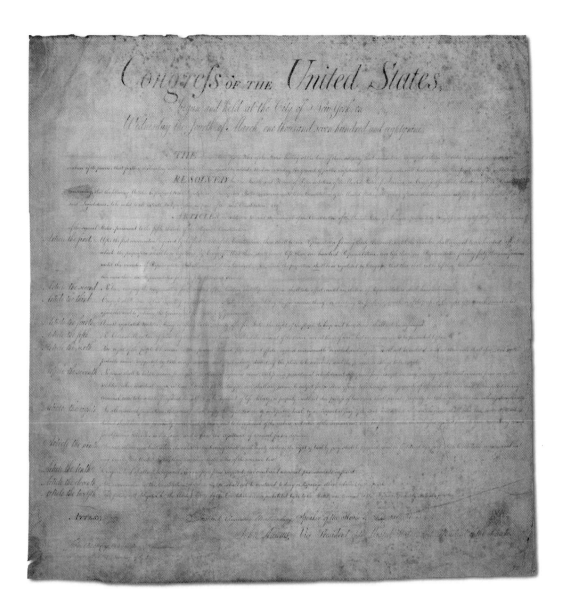

Both the Senate and the House approved this draft of the
Bill of Rights on September 28, 1789. James Madison wrote in June
1789 that he hoped these amendments would relieve any fears that
the Constitution would deprive citizens of the rights for which
they had fought.

Jefferson as his secretary of state. These two intelligent and forceful men disagreed with each other on nearly every major issue. They were Washington's principal advisers, so this meant that the administration often was split in two.

Although Madison was a friend to both Jefferson and Hamilton, he shared Jefferson's views. Hamilton was responsible for devising the financial plans of the United States. These plans included managing the nation's debt by offering creditors a chance to invest in the new nation and by taxing certain goods. Hamilton also planned to create a national bank and to promote manufacturing in America. Hamilton believed that if rich and powerful men invested in government bonds, these same men would have a vested interest in the longevity and success of the U.S. government.

Madison thought Hamilton's plans favored the rich and those who engaged in trade at the expense of independent farmers. Madison wrote that Hamilton's plans were also unfair to the veterans of the American Revolution, who had been paid for their service in promissory notes. Most veterans sold their notes to rich men and speculators for a fraction of the value. Hamilton proposed that the U.S. treasury buy back those notes at full value, which meant the rich people who owned the notes would profit. Madison was outraged by this idea. He gave speeches comparing Hamilton's plan to the financial structure of Britain with its huge debts and corruption.

Madison's attacks on Hamilton's plan led to the beginnings of the two-party political system in the United States. Those who followed Madison and Jefferson became known as Democratic-Republicans, or simply Republicans. The Republicans believed in a small national government with limited powers, no national debt, and few taxes. Those who supported Hamilton became known as Federalists. They believed in a powerful national government, a large national debt, and heavy taxes to support the government's activities.

Madison served four terms, or a total of eight years, in the House of Representatives. Madison grew weary of politics after fighting many political battles and losing nearly all of them.

In the spring of 1794, Madison was officially introduced to a beautiful widow in Philadelphia named Dolley Payne Todd. Soon the forty-three-year-old bachelor had fallen in love. Dolley's cousin, Catharine Coles, wrote Dolley in June that Madison "thinks so much of you in the day that he has lost his Tongue; at Night he Dreames of you."

Dolley was being pursued by a number of men and it was not until August that she decided to marry James Madison. After Madison heard from her, he wrote to Dolley that he had received her "precious" letter and added, "I can not express, but hope you will conceive the joy it gave me." The two were married in September 1794.

Dolley Madison was painted by Gilbert Stuart in 1804. Madison commissioned two portraits from Stuart, one of Dolley and one of himself. Madison planned to display these paintings at his Virginian home, Montpelier. Madison apparently appreciated Gilbert Stuart's work. He eventually collected and hung about six of Stuart's paintings in the drawing room at Montpelier.

By 1797, Madison wanted to retire to Montpelier. When John Adams, a Federalist, was elected president in 1796, Madison refused to run again for the House. He and Dolley returned to Virginia and to life on a tobacco plantation.

Once home, Madison concentrated on farming and on expanding the Montpelier mansion. He added rooms to separate wings of the house to give privacy to his parents and to Dolley and himself. All the while, though, Madison paid close attention to what was happening in Philadelphia.

Relations between France and the United States had deteriorated. The French resented the improved relations the United States had with Britain, with whom France was at war. The Federalists feared the influence the French Revolution might have upon the United States and the world.

In 1789, the French had begun a bloody revolution in which they overthrew and later executed King Louis XVI. The French revolutionaries drew inspiration from the American Revolution and proclaimed liberty, equality, and brotherhood for all citizens of the French republic. In the name of republicanism, the revolutionaries seized property, closed churches, and brought terror and death to thousands of people. The Federalists feared that the ideals of liberty taken to such an extreme could lead to similar acts in America and undermine the federal government.

President Adams, fearful of the unrest in Europe, began to prepare the country for a potential war. He added ships to the U.S. Navy and expanded the U.S. Army. When Congress passed the Alien Act and the Sedition Act in 1798, Adams signed them into law. The Alien Act permitted the government to imprison or deport foreigners that it considered threatening or dangerous. The Sedition Act made criticism of the government or of the president a crime. Newspaper editors were thrown in prison and a tavern keeper was arrested for making a joke about President Adams.

Madison was furious and thought both acts were unconstitutional. He carefully wrote a series of resolutions calling on the states to stand up to the federal government and to protest the acts. Madison's actual words called for the states to "interpose, for arresting the progress of the evil" posed by the Alien Act. The resolutions were introduced into the Virginia House of Delegates and were passed. The Virginia Resolutions, as they were called, were then communicated to the legislatures of the other states.

The Virginia Resolutions were considered unfavorable by seven states. Stunned by this, Madison sought election to the Virginia House of Delegates in 1799. After being elected, he wrote the Report of 1800, a long defense of the right of free speech. Both the Report of 1800 and the Virginia Resolutions were considered important expressions of Republican principles.

7. A Noble Acquisition

On February 19, 1801, a friend wrote to James Madison from Fredricksburg, Virginia, "I . . . now have the pleasure to assure You that the Voice of the People has at last been Obeyed." Thomas Jefferson had been elected president of the United States two days earlier. A tie vote in the electoral college between Jefferson and Aaron Burr had tossed the election into the House of Representatives for resolution. The Federalist and the Republican members had spent nearly one week debating before electing Jefferson. For the Republicans, this triumphant presidential election would always be known as the Revolution of 1800.

Before the election Jefferson had persuaded Madison to become his secretary of state in the new administration. Madison agreed, though he was reluctant to come out of retirement. He intended to meet Jefferson in Washington in early spring, but, in February 1801, Madison's father died. Madison remained at Montpelier to begin settling his father's estate. As the eldest of five living brothers and sisters, Madison would officially inherit Montpelier. The plantation consisted of 5,000 acres (2,024 ha) and more than one hundred slaves. This was a great responsibility, and he needed to find someone who could run Montpelier in his absence. Madison had to provide for his mother's care as well.

The Madisons finally set out for Washington, D.C., in May 1801. The city had been the capital of the United States for barely one year. About three thousand people lived in this raw forested place. Depending on the season, the streets were either dusty or muddy tracks. A few brick homes and boardinghouses clustered

William Russell Birch painted this watercolor of Washington, D.C., around 1800. At left is the north wing of the U.S. Capitol. As the Capitol was then under construction, the wing housed the Supreme Court, Congress, and the Library of Congress. Eventually, the wing would house the Senate.

together in clearings, and wooden shacks had been built helter-skelter over the hills. The President's House, which became the present-day White House, and the Capitol building, which housed the Senate and the House of Representatives, were connected by a rough road through the woods called Pennsylvania Avenue. The Madisons rented a three-story brick house on F Street, just two blocks from the President's House.

As secretary of state, James Madison was responsible for corresponding with five U.S. ministers overseas. He was also responsible for corresponding with more than fifty consuls, as the U.S. commercial representatives in port cities around the world were known. Under the president's supervision, Madison represented the United States in talks with foreign diplomats in Washington. He oversaw the Patent Office, issued federal commissions to federal officers, and kept the Great Seal of the United States. This seal was used to authenticate important state documents. Madison managed the printing and distribution of U.S. laws to the individual states. He corresponded when necessary with the governors of states and territories. To accomplish all of this, the State Department, which Madison oversaw as secretary of state, employed seven clerks and one messenger.

These were dangerous times for the United States. The country was trying to maintain its neutrality while Britain and France were still at war with each other. A neutral nation does not choose sides when other nations are in conflict with one another. These two countries had been fighting for years, with only brief periods of peace. Both France and Britain tried to ally their nation with other countries, which would thereby force those nations to join the fight. In addition, Britain tried to keep neutral countries from trading with France, and France tried to keep neutrals from trading with Britain.

International laws forbade neutral ships from carrying military stores, such as weapons, gunpowder, or uniforms. If they did, a British warship or a French privateer could seize their cargo. Sometimes the list of prohibited cargo included items such as food and drink. Many American ships were captured by privateers, and the shipowners would complain to Madison. While it was risky and difficult to carry on trade as a neutral, the financial rewards for a successful voyage were sizable. The United States soon had the largest merchant fleet of any neutral nation.

Another concern for Madison stemmed from Spain's ownership of the territories of Florida and Louisiana. A 1795 treaty between Spain and the United States, known as Pinckney's Treaty, guaranteed that Americans could deposit, or store, their goods before shipping them through the Spanish port of New Orleans. In October 1802, a Spanish official in New Orleans closed the deposit of American goods in that

This map, which highlights the course, or flow, of the Mississippi River, was created by British Lieutenant Ross after a 1765 expedition. Ross based his map on earlier French maps of the region. The Mississippi River runs through the city of New Orleans, which is marked by a blue box.

port. American farmers who in the past had sent their wheat, corn, and whiskey down the Ohio and Mississippi rivers could not get their produce to market. There was a great outcry among the westerners and talk of invading Louisiana.

In the meantime, Spain had made a secret agreement to cede Louisiana to France. When word of this leaked out, Madison and Jefferson were alarmed. Having Spain as a neighbor was not a threat. However, France was a powerful nation. If France occupied Louisiana, it would be a rival to the United States. Jefferson and Madison decided to send James Monroe, a trusted friend, on a mission to Paris to buy New Orleans and the territory along the Gulf of Mexico that was called West Florida.

When Monroe arrived in Paris in April 1803, he met with Robert R. Livingston, the U.S. minister to France. Before the two men could propose their idea to the French government, however, Napoléon Bonaparte offered to sell the entire Louisiana Territory to the United States. Napoléon feared that the British would seize New Orleans and it would then become worthless to the French. Therefore, Napoléon decided to get as much money for it as he could. The price was 15 million dollars. Monroe and Livingston accepted this offer.

The Louisiana Purchase more than doubled the size of the United States. Jefferson and Madison envisioned that these newly acquired western lands would someday be divided into states and be populated by independent farmers. They hoped that this would be an "Empire of Liberty," safe from the corruption and from the bloody wars of Europe.

As the war between France and Britain continued, Europe remained on Madison's mind. While France's vast armies ruled on land, the British navy dominated the seas. The British, therefore, posed the greatest threat to neutral trading nations. British ships stopped American merchant ships, confiscating cargo and ships if they thought them in violation of international law.

Life on a British warship was harsh, and manning all the warships in the British navy took a tremendous number of seamen. Men could be flogged for the slightest mistake. The food was bad and the work was hard. Many British seamen deserted their ships. To keep their crews at full strength, British officers impressed sailors. This means that they kidnapped sailors from other ships or abducted the sailors while they were in port and then

In this 1884 engraving, which was based on an illustration by Howard Pyle, a British naval officer examines a group of American seamen for impressment into the British navy. Some American officials suggested that American sailors carry certificates proving that they were Americans and not deserters from the British navy.

took them on board British ships. Once the ship set sail, there was no opportunity to escape, and the sailor had no choice except to enter the British navy. This practice of impressment made Americans extremely angry.

British officers impressed many Americans because it was often hard to tell an American sailor from a British one, as an American might be an English, Irish, or Scottish person who had immigrated to the United States. Sometimes the British would stop an American ship in mid-ocean and take any crew members they wanted.

Complaints from angry Americans flooded the State Department. Madison went to the British minister in Washington and tried to negotiate an end to this practice. The British refused to cooperate.

By 1807, France and Britain were determined to halt each other's trade. France ordered that any ship stopping at a British port or carrying British goods could be taken as a lawful prize. Britain ordered that any ship trading with a European port was required to stop in a British port and obtain a license. These orders meant that any American ship trading anywhere in Europe was liable to be taken by either the French or the British.

Madison believed that the United States could force the French and the British to take back these orders if American goods, such as wheat, tobacco, and flour, were denied to them. He and Jefferson proposed an embargo, or a plan that prevented American ships from leaving any American port to trade anywhere. An embargo would save American ships from seizure and, by creating shortages of American goods in Europe, would force the British and the French to reverse their orders.

The Embargo Act of 1807 was a failure. American merchants did not like it. They preferred the risks of trade to watching their ships remain in the harbor. American goods were smuggled into British Canada and into Spanish Florida. Local officials had to police the embargo and that made them unpopular. Furthermore, other nations took over the shipping of goods that had previously been transported by American ships. Congress passed a law ending the embargo in March 1809.

8. Walking the Line

The debate over the Embargo Act split the Republican party into thirds. When Jefferson decided not to run for a third term, each group supported a different candidate for the presidential election of 1808. One group wanted to nominate the vice president, George Clinton. Another wanted to nominate James Monroe. A third thought that James Madison would be the best candidate.

Presidential nominations were made by party caucuses that were held around the country. A caucus is a meeting of party members who hold political office, such as senators and representatives. Madison was chosen in the January 1808 caucus held in Washington. In the election of 1808, Madison beat Clinton, Monroe, and the Federalist candidate, Charles Cotesworth Pinckney, by an impressive margin.

Opposite: Gilbert Stuart painted this portrait of Madison around 1805. At his inauguration James Madison wore a suit that was made in Connecticut. By not ordering a suit from a fashionable European tailor, Madison showed his support for American manufacturers.

On March 4, 1809, James Madison was inaugurated as the fourth president of the United States. Before a large crowd of dignitaries and guests, Madison gave his inaugural address. He "was extremely pale and trembled excessively when he first began to speak, but [he] soon gained confidence and spoke audibly," wrote one observer. In his address Madison reviewed the past course of the nation and then proposed a list of principles that would guide his administration. Madison hoped "to cherish peace and friendly intercourse with all nations having correspondent dispositions . . . [and] to maintain sincere neutrality towards belligerent [warlike] nations."

A reception followed the inauguration and a grand ball was held that evening. This was the first inaugural ball in American history and no doubt it was Dolley Madison's idea. Four hundred guests were invited. Dolley wore a pale yellow velvet gown and a matching turban with feather plumes. Although Dolley and James did not dance, for she had been brought up a Quaker, their guests danced until midnight.

The ball heralded a big change in Washington social life. Jefferson was a widower and had usually entertained his guests by hosting small dinners. Dolley and James Madison wanted to open up the President's House to more people and to make it gay and festive. They desired a place where people of all political opinions could come and discuss the events of the day. Dolley repainted the public rooms and bought new furniture, mirrors, and drapes. She wanted the President's House to be worthy of the president.

Once the house was refurbished, she invited the public, that is, anyone who wished to come, to an open house every Wednesday evening. Dolley called these events her "Drawing Room evenings," but so many people came to them that they became known as Squeezes. Some people came elegantly dressed, while others arrived in their everyday clothes and dirty boots. The first lady and the president made all guests feel welcome.

This drawing by L. M. Glackens accompanied the 1901 poem "The Reign of Doll[e]y Madison." Dolley Madison, depicted at the center of the image, offers a gentleman a glass of wine. Guests at the Madisons' Wednesday night Squeezes helped themselves to a buffet of ice cream, cookies, and fruit, as well as to beverages such as wine and punch.

President Madison was trying to walk a fine line between bowing before British and French aggression and not provoking either of these two nations to war. The Federalists wanted Madison to give in to the British, while many Republicans thought he should declare war. Madison wanted to do neither.

In March 1809, the Embargo Act was replaced by a Non-Intercourse Act, which forbade British and French ships from entering U.S. ports. When this measure failed, the 1810 Macon's Bill No. 1 promised to renew trade with either Britain or France if these nations would allow the United States to trade freely. Congress soon substituted this bill for Macon's Bill No. 2, which opened trade to France and Britain, but which threatened nonintercourse with one nation if the other lifted its ban on U.S. trade. For example, if Britain stopped interfering with U.S. trade then the United States would halt its trade with France. These complicated measures were all attempts to solve the problem of foreign attacks on U.S. ships.

Much to Madison's surprise, he learned in September 1810 that the French had relaxed their measures against U.S. trade. This was enough, Madison thought, to impose nonintercourse with Britain if that country did not relax its orders to impede American trade as well.

Madison's offer to the British was met with arrogance and an increase in the number of impressments and captured U.S. ships. The president had no choice but to prepare the nation for war. In the congressional session that began in November 1811, Madison called for an expanded army and navy and for the stockpiling of military supplies. He also told the British minister in Washington, Augustus John Foster, that this was Britain's last chance to revoke their hostile orders.

By May 1812, it was clear that the British would not relent. The danger to Britain from the French emperor Napoléon Bonaparte easily outweighed the threat of war with the United States. Furthermore, Britain's fight against France included the fight to control neutral trade.

On June 1, 1812, James Madison sent a message to Congress asking it to consider the question of going to war or maintaining peace with Britain. Although the president had decided that war was necessary, only Congress could declare war. A secret session of the House of Representatives voted 79–49 in favor of war on June 4. On June 17, the Senate, by a vote of 19–13, agreed. The War of 1812 had begun.

9. The United States Stands Up to Britain

The War of 1812 was the first war the United States fought under its new Constitution. The U.S. president is commander in chief of all the armed forces, including the U.S. Army, the U.S. Navy, and the U.S. Marines. How the war is conducted is the president's responsibility.

President James Madison wanted to strike quickly against Britain while the British were fighting the French in Europe. He ordered the navy, consisting of six frigates and a handful of smaller ships, to protect American shipping and to fight the enemy if they could meet the British on equal terms. American frigates carried forty-four cannons and were no match for some of Britain's largest ships, which carried seventy-six cannons.

Next the president ordered the army and the state militias to attack Canada, which was a British colony, from three places: Detroit in the Michigan Territory; Niagara, New York; and the Champlain Valley in northern New York, near Montreal. The British had only about three thousand regular troops on hand to guard the long Canadian frontier, although they had strong allies in the Native Americans of the Northwest. Madison hoped that U.S. forces could take Canada before the British could send reinforcements.

The three campaigns were disastrous. General William Hull not only failed to take his objective, but also lost Detroit and surrendered his entire army of two thousand men. General Alexander Smyth advanced into Canada on the Niagara Peninsula, only to be thrown back by the British after the Americans were defeated at the Battle of Queenstown Heights. General Henry Dearborn had advanced just a short distance toward Montreal before he turned his army around and went into winter quarters, not far from where he had started.

Madison was disheartened. Not only had the United States failed to take Canada, giving the British time to reinforce their army in North America, but American defeats also fueled critics of the war and Madison's political opponents. The president was facing another election that fall. Despite the miserable military campaigns of 1812, Madison was reelected to the presidency that same year by a vote of 128 to 89.

There was other good news as well. The navy had been successful in protecting American shipping and had beaten the enemy three times in single-ship combats. The victories of the American warships *Wasp*, *Constitution*, and *United States* proved that the

American navy was an equal to the British navy in seamanship and gunnery, if not in numbers.

That winter Madison began to prepare for the campaigns of 1813. He had learned from the defeats of 1812 that only naval control of the Great Lakes, which would cut British supply lines, and the occupation of Montreal would win the war. Madison ordered Master Commandant Oliver Hazard Perry to Erie, Pennsylvania, to build a naval fleet that would control Lake Erie. He also ordered Captain Isaac Chauncey to do the same from Lake Ontario. Meanwhile, Madison called on Congress to expand the army and create more senior officers. The president wanted to retire some of the older generals and to promote younger, more energetic men to command. He also asked his secretaries of war and navy to resign and then chose other men that he hoped would be more organized.

Oliver Hazard Perry, painted by T. Young in 1803, left his home in Rhode Island at age thirteen to join the U.S. Navy.

Unfortunately, Madison could do little about the heated opposition of the Federalist Party. The Federalists called the conflict Mr. Madison's War and wanted no part of it. The Federalists were strongest in

New England, especially in the states of Massachusetts and Connecticut. Those states refused to muster their militias, and obstructed army recruiters within their borders. There was even talk of disunion. Such actions convinced the British that the United States could not continue the war for long.

The situation in the spring of 1813 did not look promising. Despite the capture of York, or present-day Toronto, Canada, American forces made no progress on the other fronts. When Czar Alexander I of Russia offered to mediate talks between the United States and Britain, Madison accepted and sent a number of commissioners to St. Petersburg, Russia, to represent the United States in these negotiations.

The British, meanwhile, had already sent a fleet of ships to blockade American ports and to attack and plunder areas on the Atlantic coast. The British attacked towns in and around the Chesapeake Bay and burned Havre de Grace, Maryland, to the ground. Americans were outraged at the inability of U.S. forces to stop the British.

By early June 1813, two years of worry and constant work took a toll on the president. He became gravely ill with "bilious fever," which was probably a form of malaria. Madison did not leave his bed until mid-July. Even then he was so weak that Dolley wrote, "I watch over him as I would an infant." When the president was finally strong enough to make the trip, the Madisons went home to Montpelier for a two-month vacation that was long overdue.

In September came word that Oliver Hazard Perry had defeated a British fleet on Lake Erie. "We have met the enemy and they are ours," Perry wrote. Master Commandant Perry was quickly promoted to the rank of captain for his leadership during the battle.

U.S. control of the lake meant that the British had to evacuate Detroit in the Michigan Territory. In October 1813, General William Henry Harrison and his army pursued the British north and defeated them at the Battle of the Thames. The victory ended British and Indian power in the Northwest. Madison also learned that, although the British had refused

This drawing from around 1814 by Thomas Birch dramatizes the Battle of Lake Erie during the War of 1812. When Oliver Hazard Perry sailed the U.S. fleet into battle against the British, his ship carried a blue flag that displayed the words "Don't Give Up The Ship."

directing the packing of official papers and public property, such as the silver plate and red velvet drapes, into a wagon. At the last moment Dolley had the famous Gilbert Stuart portrait of George Washington cut from its frame. The first lady gave the portrait to two gentlemen for safekeeping and then she hurried off across the Potomac River to Virginia.

Madison followed. The couple finally reunited on August 25 at Wiley's Tavern in Virginia. The president then went on to Brookeville, Maryland, in search of the army and its commanders. After conferring with army leaders on August 26, Madison returned to Washington the next day. He arrived to find the President's House destroyed, its fire-streaked walls looking forlorn. The Capitol was also a shell. Madison quickly found other quarters and then he went about the city, James Monroe later wrote, "animating and encouraging the troops and citizens not to despair." The president knew that it was important that the government quickly return to normal, both to inspire Americans and to defy the British.

Although the president's spirits rose with American victories in September 1814, British and American peace negotiations at Ghent, in the Austrian Netherlands, present-day Belgium, were not going well.

Next spread: The Taking of the City of Washington in America was engraved by G. Thompson in London and published on October 14, 1814. The British set fire to several government buildings in Washington, D.C., on August 24, 1814.

Dolley Madison instructed her staff to rescue this portrait of George Washington, painted by Gilbert Stuart, before the British burned down the President's House in 1814. The U.S. government had purchased this portrait of Washington in 1800.

In addition, Federalists had met in Hartford, Connecticut, to discuss the possibility that New England might separate itself from the United States. Worst of all, a British army of about ten thousand men was headed for New Orleans.

The winter of 1814–1815 was an agonizing one for Madison. The outcome of the war hung on events in Ghent, Hartford, and New Orleans. Madison had laid down the groundwork for victory and peace. He had promoted Andrew Jackson to the command at New Orleans. He had sent America's best negotiators to represent the United States at Ghent. Finally, Madison could only hope that the Federalists at Hartford would remember that their country came before their political ambitions. A fellow Virginian, William Wirt, who visited Madison that winter, wrote that the president looked "miserably shattered and woe-begone."

On January 9, 1815, the resolves of the Hartford Convention reached Madison. The convention of New England Federalists had not proposed disunion but had postponed their decision and had called for another meeting that summer. Then, on February 4, the city rang with the news of Jackson's victory at New Orleans. The battle had taken place one month earlier. The victory was so complete that it drove the British back to their ships with no thought of renewing the invasion.

Ten days later the peace treaty from Ghent arrived. The treaty had been signed in December on the basis of *status quo ante bellum*, which is Latin for the same situation the two nations had found themselves in before the war. This meant that neither side had gained any territory or special privileges because of the war. Much had changed, though.

The United States had won a second war for independence. Madison had shown that the nation could fight a war within the framework of the U.S. Constitution. The young American republic had fought a great European power on equal terms.

10. Montpelier and Retirement

The last years of James Madison's presidency were years of triumph and goodwill. The bitterness between the Republicans and the Federalists diminished with the successful end to the war. The winter months were filled with balls, parties, and Dolley's famous "Squeezes." President Madison's popularity rose as the nation realized what he had accomplished. The president and the nation had stood up to the British and had survived.

James Monroe, Madison's friend and secretary of state, was elected president in 1816. Monroe was inaugurated on March 4, 1817, and Madison retired from public office for good. The Madisons packed up their Washington household and traveled on a steamboat down the Potomac River to Aquia Creek, to meet their carriage for the overland trip to Montpelier. James K. Paulding, who was along for the journey, wrote that Madison, finally "freed from the cares of Public Life . . . was as playful as a child; talked and jested with everybody on board."

At home at Montpelier, the Madisons settled into the relaxed rhythms of plantation life. For the first time in forty years, Madison's life revolved around the seasons rather than around politics. Plowing, planting, weeding, and harvesting crops of tobacco, wheat, and corn were his main concerns. He was responsible for managing the plantation and for directing the work of more than one hundred slaves. Every morning Madison rode out on his favorite horse, Liberty, to inspect the ongoing work on his farms and to check the health of the cattle, sheep, and hogs. Without a government salary, the plantation had to support all those who lived at Montpelier.

There were always visitors at Montpelier. Except for during the brief Virginian winters, the house, as Dolley once wrote, was always "full of company, relations, connections, neighbors, and strangers." At the Fourth of July dinner in 1816, there were more than eighty gentlemen and a few ladies seated at one table on Montpelier's back lawn. The Madisons also visited their neighbors on surrounding plantations and once or twice per year they traveled to Jefferson's home at Monticello.

Winters were a time of calm. Dolley read the latest novels and poetry, while James read history and the numerous newspapers to which he still subscribed. The couple also liked to play chess. During the first winter of his retirement, Madison began collecting, arranging, and editing his personal papers.

Madison knew that he had lived through and participated in historic events. Over the years he had corresponded with the great men of the American Revolution and with the individuals who had founded the Republic. There was hardly an important figure of that period with whom Madison had not exchanged a letter. In addition, there were the notes that Madison had taken during his years in the Continental Congress of 1780–1783 and the Constitutional Convention of 1787. Madison knew that his notes written at the Convention were the most complete record of what had taken place there. He intended that they be published after his death, so that future Americans would be able to learn about how their nation was founded.

The work was slow and tedious. To Dolley, who helped him, the task seemed endless. After three winters of work she complained to a friend that "the business appears to accumalate as he proceeds—so that I calculate its out-lasting my patience." Seven years later Dolley and James were still at it. In fact, Dolley would finally complete the work after James's death.

Another project of Madison's retirement years was to help his friend Jefferson build the University of

---

Next Page: This structure, which was called the garden temple, was constructed at Montpelier around 1811. The temple was used to mask an ice house that was set into the ground beneath the floor of the temple. In the hot summer months, blocks of ice were brought up from the ice house to make ice cream and cold beverages.

Thomas Jefferson recorded the May 5, 1817, minutes, or record of what transpired, at one of the first meetings of the Board of Visitors for Central College, which was renamed the University of Virginia in 1819. James Madison was a board member and signed the document. The Board resolved that Jefferson and John H. Cocke were authorized to make the decisions and direct the spending of money for the college.

Virginia in Charlottesville. Madison participated in the planning of the college and was a member of its first Board of Visitors. He helped Jefferson in everything from selecting the first professors to making up a list of books on religion to be purchased for the library. When Jefferson died in 1826, Madison became the university's second rector. He remained in that post until 1834, when he became too sick to hold it. In his will Madison donated most of his books as well as a cash bequest to the university's library.

In 1829, Madison was called one last time into public service. He was elected as a delegate from Orange County to a state convention in Richmond called to redraft the Virginia Constitution. Here he consulted with the other delegates and presented his ideas to the convention. This was to be Madison's last public speech.

Despite his busy life and public honors, all was not well at Montpelier. There had been a series of dreadful tobacco and wheat harvests in the 1820s. In addition, European demand for those crops had fallen since the end of the Napoleonic Wars, which drove down the price of those two commodities. The plantation's income was falling. Whatever money the Madisons had saved during Madison's presidency had been spent in the first few years after they returned to Montpelier. To support Montpelier and themselves, the Madisons had to borrow money from a bank.

This portrait of John Payne Todd from around 1830 was probably based on a work by Henry Kurtz. When Todd died in 1851, he admitted to having been "my own worst enemy."

If that was not troublesome enough, Dolley Madison's son by her first marriage, John Payne Todd, was a drunk and a gambler.

Dolley Madison was painted by her niece, Mary Estelle Elizabeth
Cutts, around 1840. Dolley, who would live until 1849, was asked in
1844 to wire the first private message at a public demonstration of
Samuel Morse's telegraph machine. This was a great honor.

manufacture cotton cloth, wanted the tariff because it protected their growing industry. The tax made foreign cloth more expensive than American cloth. Some southern states, such as South Carolina, refused to pay the tariff and, in fact, threatened to secede from the Union. Moreover, they quoted James Madison's Virginia Resolutions of 1798 in their arguments.

Madison was aware that southerners had used what he had written in the Virginia Resolutions in their arguments. He did not agree with them and thought they had misinterpreted what he had written. Madison had said that the states should find means to protest federal measures if they thought them unjust, but he had never called for states to leave the Union.

James Madison explained his position in a letter to Cabell, who had the letter published in the newspapers. Although some southerners were swayed by Madison's arguments, others thought that Madison had betrayed them, or had grown too old. Madison himself wrote to a friend in 1831, "[that] having outlived so many of my contemporaries I ought not to forget that I may be thought to have outlived myself."

Though the tariff crisis finally passed, the plantation owner and former president worried about the great issue that divided the north and the south, slavery. "The magnitude of this evil among us is so deeply felt, and so universally acknowledged," he wrote, "that no merit could be greater than that of devising a satisfactory remedy for it." Yet Madison had no answer for the evils of slavery beyond colonization, which was the idea that the state or federal government would buy slaves from their owners and send them to Africa. Madison never believed that the two races could live peaceably and side by side in freedom. Because he worried about his wife's financial well-being, Madison felt that he could not afford to free his slaves after his death.

What worried Madison the most as he lay weak and bedridden in his final years was not the federal tariff or slavery, but the future of the Union. In 1834, Madison wrote what he called Advice to My Country. "The advice nearest to my heart and deepest in my convictions is that the Union of the States be cherished and perpetuated."

When he died on June 28, 1836, at the age of eighty-five, James Madison was the last survivor of those who had attended the Constitutional Convention. He was laid to rest in the family cemetery at Montpelier. Dolley, who through poverty was later forced to sell Montpelier and move to Washington, lived on until 1849.

How do we remember James Madison? In Washington, D.C., George Washington's great memorial soars high above the Mall, and Thomas Jefferson's memorial is reflected in a giant pool surrounded by flowering cherry trees. Millions of Americans visit these sites every year. James Madison has a memorial,

This is the original 1787 copy of the Constitution of the United States. In 1829, Madison wrote, "The happy Union of these States is a wonder; their Constitution a miracle; their example the hope of Liberty throughout the world."

too, but his is not made of marble. Madison's memorial is written in parchment. His enduring legacy is the U.S. Constitution, with its Bill of Rights, as well as the continued existence of the Union he worked so hard to create and sustain over his long and eventful life.

Timeline

1751	James Madison is born on March 16 at Port Conway, Virginia.
1769–72	Madison studies at the College of New Jersey at Princeton.
1776	Madison attends the Virginia Convention as a delegate from Orange County.
1778–79	Madison serves as a member of the Virginia Council of State.
1780–83	Madison serves as a Virginian member of the Continental Congress.
1784–86	Madison attends the Virginia General Assembly as an Orange County delegate.
1786	Madison attends the Annapolis Convention in September.
1787	Madison attends the Constitutional Convention and writes essays for *The Federalist*.
1787–88	Madison is a member of the Continental Congress.
1788	Madison serves in the Virginia Ratifying Convention.
1789–97	Madison serves in the U.S. House of Representatives.
1789	Madison sponsors the Bill of Rights.
1794	James Madison marries Dolley Payne Todd in September.
1797	Madison retires to Montpelier.
1799	Madison serves in the Virginia General Assembly.
1801	Madison is appointed secretary of state.
1809	Madison is inaugurated as the fourth U.S. president.

1812	Madison is elected to a second term as president. War is declared against Britain.
1814	The British burn Washington, D.C.
1815	War with Britain ends.
1817	Madison retires to Montpelier.
1826	Madison becomes rector of the University of Virginia.
1829	Madison attends the Virginia Constitutional Convention.
1836	James Madison dies at Montpelier on June 28.

Glossary

amendment (uh-MEND-ment) An addition or a change to the U.S. Constitution.

armory (ARM-ree) A place where arms and ammunition are stored.

arresting (uh-REST-ing) Stopping, or bringing something to a halt.

Board of Visitors (BORD UV VIH-zih-terz) A committee that is appointed by the governor, which decides overall policy for the University of Virginia.

casualties (KA-zhul-teez) The number of soldiers killed, wounded, or captured in battle.

collaboration (kuh-la-buh-RAY-shun) A partnership in which people work jointly toward a common goal.

commissioned (kuh-MIH-shund) To have been asked to do a job.

commodities (kuh-MAH-duh-teez) Things that are bought or sold, especially products of agriculture.

confiscating (KON-fih-skayt-ing) Legally taking property away.

congregations (kahn-gruh-GAY-shunz) Groups of people who have come together for reasons of faith.

constituent (kun-STICH-went) One of a group who elects another to represent him or her in a public office.

convened (kun-VEEND) To have assembled together as a group.

delegate (DEH-lih-get) A representative elected to attend a political gathering.

deliberated (dih-LIH-buh-rayt-ed) To have examined and discussed something with great care.

deport (dih-PORT) To send out of a country.

devise (dih-VYZ) To plan or scheme.

diligently (DIH-lih-jent-lee) Characterized by steady, earnest, and energetic effort.

frigate (FRIH-git) A small, swift vessel that could be equipped as a warship or transport.

inalienable (ih-NAYL-yeh-nuh-bul) Describing something, such as a right or a privilege, that cannot be surrendered.

intense (in-TENTS) Concentrated.

interpose (in-TER-pohz) To come between.

intervene (in-ter-VEEN) To interfere in someone else's affairs.

kindled (KIN-duld) To have inspired.

levied (LEH-veed) To have authorized the collection of money.

maladies (MA-luh-deez) More than one illness or disease.

militias (muh-LIH-shuhz) Groups of volunteer or citizen soldiers who are organized to assemble in emergencies.

muster (MUHS-ter) To bring together.

nonintercourse (NON-in-ter-kors) Banning trade with another country.

nurseries (NURS-reez) Places where plants and trees are raised and sold.

orator (OR-uh-tur) A skilled public speaker.

parchment (PARCH-ment) The hide of an animal that was prepared to be written on for use in important documents.

petition (puh-TIH-shun) A formal request to ask for something to be done.

Piedmont (PEED-mont) Literally, at the foot of the mountains. This is the area between Tidewater, Virginia, and the mountains.

plantation (plan-TAY-shun) A very large farm where crops were grown.

postponed (pohst-POHND) To have delayed or pushed back something.

promissory notes (PRAH-mih-sor-ee NOHTS) Checks, or a promise to pay.

rector (REK-ter) The head of a university.

remonstrance (rih-MON-strihns) A document that presents an argument against something.

republicanism (rih-PUH-blih-kuh-nih-zem) The belief that, in a government, power should rest with people elected by citizens.

requisition (reh-kwuh-ZIH-shun) To call upon an organization to provide something.

retaliated (rih-TA-lee-ayt-id) To have taken revenge.

revisions (rih-VIH-zhun) Changed accounts of something, usually made to improve it.

rigors (RIH-gurz) Challenges or difficulties.

satirized (SA-tih-ryzd) To have used wit or sarcasm in making fun of something.

secular (SEH-kyuh-lur) Pertaining to the world, and not related to religion or religious beliefs.

silver plate (SIL-ver PLAYT) Eating utensils and plates that have been coated with silver.

Additional Resources

To learn more about James Madison, check out the following books and Web sites:

Books

Shulman, Holly C. and David B. Mattern. *Dolley Madison: Her Life, Letters, and Legacy*. New York: Rosen PowerPlus Books, 2002.

Wilbur, C. Keith. *The Revolutionary Soldier, 1775–1783*. Old Saybrook, Connecticut: The Globe Pequot Press, 1993.

Web Sites

Due to the changing nature of Internet links, PowerPlus Books has developed an online list of Web sites related to the subject of this book. This site is updated regularly. Please use this link to access the list:
www.powerkidslinks.com/lalt/jmadison/

Bibliography

Hutchinson, William T. and William M. E. Rachal, et al eds. *The Papers of James Madison*. Chicago and Charlottesville, Virginia: University of Chicago Press (vols. 1–10) and University of Virginia Press (vols. 11–17; Secretary of State Series, 6 vols. to date; Presidential Series, 4 vols. to date), [1962], 1991.

James Madison Center, James Madison University, *James Madison: His Legacy*: http://www.jmu.edu/madison/.

Ketcham, Ralph. *James Madison: A Biography*. Charlottesville, Virginia: University of Virginia Press, 1990.

Rakove, Jack. *James Madison and the Creation of the American Republic*. New York: Longman Press, 1990.

Rutland, Robert Allen. *James Madison: The Founding Father*. Columbia: The University of Missouri Press, 1997.

Stagg, J.C.A. *Mr. Madison's War: Politics, Diplomacy, and Warfare in the Early American Republic, 1783–1830*. Princeton, New Jersey: Princeton University Press, 1983.

Index

About the Author

David B. Mattern is senior associate editor of *The Papers of James Madison* and research associate professor at the University of Virginia. He is the editor of several volumes of *The Papers of James Madison*, as well as author of *Benjamin Lincoln and the American Revolution*. He is co-author (with Holly C. Shulman) of *Dolley Madison: Her Life, Letters, and Legacy*.

About the Consultant

Kenneth M. Clark is the administrator of the Orange County Historical Society, Inc., in Orange, Virginia. He is the historian and former president of the James Madison Museum, also in Orange. Since he grew up in the shadow of Montpelier, Ken has had a lifelong interest in the Madisons and Montpelier. In 1987, he fulfilled a dream by becoming a tour guide at James Madison's Montpelier. Ken has consulted on numerous publications on the Madisons.

Primary Sources

Cover. *James Madison*, detail from painting, 1816, John Vanderlyn, The White House Collection, White House Historical Association, Background Signed Copy of the Constitution of the United States; Miscellaneous Papers of the Continental Congress, 1774–1789; 1774–1789, National Archives and Records Administration. **Page 4.** *James Madison*, painting, 1792, Charles Willson Peale, The Thomas Gilcrease Institute of American History and Art, Tulsa, OK. **Page 9.** *James Madison's House at Montpelier, Virginia, 1818*, watercolor and gouache, Baroness Hyde de Neuville, Reunion des Musees Nationaux/Art Resource, NY. **Page 10.** *4 scenes showing curing, airing, and storing of tobacco, Tidewater, Virginia, pre-1800*, engraving, 1800, William Tatham, Library of Congress Prints and Photographs Division. **Page 11.** *James Madison Sr.*, painting, 1799, Charles Peale Polk, Belle Grove Plantation, Middletown, VA. **Page 12.** *Eleanor Rose Conway Madison*, painting, ca. 1799, Charles Peale Polk, Belle Grove Plantation, Middletown, VA. **Page 16.** *An East Perspective View of the City of Philadelphia, in the Province of Pennsylvania*, engraving, ca. 1752, based on a work by George Heap, The Phelps Stokes Collection, Miriam and Ira D. Wallach Division of Art, Prints, and Photographs, the New York Public Library, Astor, Lenox, and Tilden Foundations. **Page 17.** *John Witherspoon*, painting, 1794. Rembrandt Peale, based on a 1787 work by Charles Willson Peale, National Portrait Gallery, Smithsonian Institution/Art Resorce. **Page 18.** "The Solar System from Copernicus," drawing, ca. 1770, James Madison, Library of Congress Manuscript Division. **Page 19.** Madison's diploma from the College of New Jersey, 1772, Library of Congress Manuscript Division. Page 23. Petition against General Assessment, December 25, 1776, Library of Congress Manuscript Division. **Page 27.** *Leaders of the Continental Congress—John Adams, Gouverneur Morris, Alexander Hamilton, Thomas Jefferson*, ca. 1894, Augustus Tholey, Prints and Photographs Division, Library of Congress. **Page 30.** Continental currency, January 14, 1779, reproduced with permission from the Robert H. Gore, Jr. Numismatic Collection, Department of Special Collections, University of Notre Dame Libraries. **Page 34.** *Patrick Henry Arguing the Parson's Cause at the Hanover County Courthouse*, painting, ca. 1834, George Cooke, Virginia Historical Society. **Page 36.** Memorial and Remonstrance, holograph document, 1785, James Madison, Library of Congress Manuscript Division. **Page 41.** The Virginia Plan, holograph document, May 29, 1787, handwritten by George Washington, Library of Congress Manuscript Division. **Page 42–43.** *The Constitutional Convention of 1787*, painting, ca. 1872, Thomas Pritchard Rossiter, Independence National Historic Park. **Page 46.** *Alexander Hamilton*, painting, finished in 1805, John Trumbull, The White House Collection, courtesy of the White House Historical Association. **Page 47.** *John Jay*, painting, ca. 1843, Henry Peters Gray, based on an earlier 1794 work by Gilbert Stuart, Collection of the Supreme Court of the United States. **Page 48.** *The Federalist: A Collection of Essays, Written in Favour of the New Constitution*, vol. 1, 1788, John Jay, James Madison, Alexander Hamilton, Library of Congress Rare Books and Special Collections Division. **Page 53.** The Bill of Rights, September 28, 1789, holograph on vellum, John Beckley copy, NARA. **Page 56.** *Dolley Madison*, painting, 1804, Gilbert Stuart, White House Collection, the White House Historical Association. **Page 60.** *A view of the Capitol of Washington before it was burnt down by the British*, watercolor and drawing, ca 1800, William Russell Birch, Library of Congress Prints and Photographs Division. **Page 63.** *Course of the river Mississippi, from the Balise to Fort Chartres; taken on an expedition to the Illinois, in the latter end of the year*

1765, map, 1772, Lieut. Ross, Robert Sayer, Library of Congress Geography and Map Division. **Page 65.** *Impressment of American seamen*, engraving, April 1884, Howard Pyle, Library of Congress, Prints and Photographs Division. **Page 69.** *James Madison*, painting, ca. 1805, Gilbert Stuart, Burstein Collection/CORBIS. **Page 71.** *The Reign of Dolly Madison*, drawing, April 24, 1901, L. M. Glackens, Library of Congress Prints and Photographs Division. **Page 76.** *Oliver Hazard Perry*, painting, 1803, T. Young, U.S. Navy Art Collection. **Page 78.** *Perry's victory*, drawing, ca. 1814, Thomas Birch, Library of Congress Prints and Photographs Division. **Page 79.** *A boxing match, or Another bloody nose for John Bull*, etching with watercolor, 1813, William Charles, Library of Congress. **Page 82–83.** *The Taking of the City of Washington in America*, engraving, October 14, 1814, G. Thompson, Library of Congress Prints and Photographs Division. **Page 84.** *George Washington*, painting, 1800, Gilbert Stuart, White House Collection, courtesy the White House Historical Association. **Page 90.** Garden Temple at Montpelier, constructed in 1811, photo courtesy of Dr. Ted Sherwin, The Montpelier Foundation, at James Madison's Montpelier. **Page 91.** Minutes of the first meeting of the Board of Visitors of Central College, manuscript in Thomas Jefferson's handwriting, May 5, 1817, signed by Thomas Jefferson, James Monroe, and James Madison, University of Virginia Albert & Shirley Small Special Collections Library. **Page 92.** *John Payne Todd*, portrait, circa 1830, possibly based on an earlier miniature by Henry Kurtz, General Research Division, New York Public Library Astor, Lenox, and Tilden Foundations. **Page 93.** *James Madison*, painting, 1833, James B. Longacre, Madison Collection of the James Madison Museum, Orange, VA. **Page 95.** *Dolley Payne Todd Madison*, watercolor, ca. 1840, Mary Estelle Elizabeth Cutts, White House Collection, courtesy of the White House Historical Association. **Page 98.** See cover.

Credits

Photo Credits

Cover, pp. 46, 56, 84, 95, The White House Collection, courtesy of the White House Historical Association; cover background, pp. 53, 98, National Archives and Records Administration; p. 4 The Thomas Gilcrease Institute of American History and Art, Tulsa, Oklahoma; p. 9 © Reunion des Musees Nationaux / Art Resource, NY; pp. 10, 18, 19, 23, 27, 36, 41, 48, 50, 60, 63, 65, 71, 78, 79, 82-83, Library of Congress; pp. 11, 12 Belle Grove Plantation, Middletown, VA. A historic property of the National Trust for Historic Preservation; p. 16 the Phelps Stokes Collection, Miriam and Ira D. Wallach Division of Art, Prints, and Photographs, the New York Public Library, Astor Lenox, and Tilden Foundations; p. 17 © National Portrait Gallery, Smithsonian Institution / Art Resource, NY; p. 30 Reproduced with permission from the Robert H. Gore, Jr. Numismatic Collection, Department of Special Collections, University of Notre Dame Libraries; p. 34 Virginia Historical Society; pp. 42-43 Courtesy Independence National Historical Park; p. 47 Collection of the Supreme Court of the United States; p. 69 © Burstein Collection/CORBIS; p. 76 US Navy Art Collection; p. 90 Photograph by Dr. Ted Sherwin, courtesy of The Montpelier Foundation, James Madison's Montpelier; p. 91 University of Virginia Albert & Shirley Small Special Collections Library; p. 92 General Research Division, New York Public Library Astor, Lenox, and Tilden Foundations; p. 93 Madison Collection of the James Madison Museum, Orange, VA.

Project Editor Daryl Heller

Series Design Laura Murawski

Layout Design Corinne L. Jacob
Maria E. Melendez

Photo Researcher Jeffrey Wendt